Microsoft® SQL Server™ 2008

A BEGINNER'S GUIDE

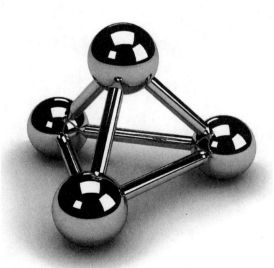

About the Author

Dušan Petković is a professor in the Department of Computer Science at the Polytechnic in Rosenheim, Germany. He is the author of *SQL Server 7: A Beginner's Guide, SQL Server 2000: A Beginner's Guide*, and *Microsoft SQL Server 2005: A Beginner's Guide*, and is a frequent contributor to *SQL Server Magazine*.

About the Technical Editor

Todd Meister has been using Microsoft technologies for over ten years. He's been a technical editor on over 40 titles ranging from SQL Server to the .NET Framework. In addition, he is an assistant director for computing services at Ball State University in Muncie, Indiana. He lives with his wife, Kimberly, and their four children in central Indiana. Contact Todd at tmeister@sycamoresolutions.com.